Beginner's Guide to Keepa Graphs

By Honey Woods

Table of Contents:

INTRODUCTION TO KEEPA

One of the best resources available to provide sellers with reliable information on the historical sales and pricing of a product on Amazon is Keepa. While the sales rank of an item can give you a snapshot view of how well a product is selling, to make a more well-informed decision, you really need a tool that can give you more information; and Keepa is that tool. You can sign up for an account with Keepa at keepa.com and access it for a small monthly fee or save some money by signing up for a yearly subscription. Please note that it is billed in Euros.

Keepa can be accessed through both website and Facebook messenger, but when doing quick product research on an existing listing from a desktop, the Chrome extension makes using it a seamless process. There is also a phone app that has recently been made available, but many still choose to use the site from a phone's browser as it is more user friendly and also a seamless transition if you are used to how it works when doing online arbitrage.

The main things you want to focus on when reading a Keepa chart are the sales rank, pricing, and the seller count. While there are MANY other useful features in Keepa, for most, information overload can easily occur. For the purposes of this reference, we're going to keep it simple. As you grow your business and become more familiar with Keepa, you can expand your knowledge of the powerful tool that it is.

BASIC PARTS OF A KEEPA GRAPH

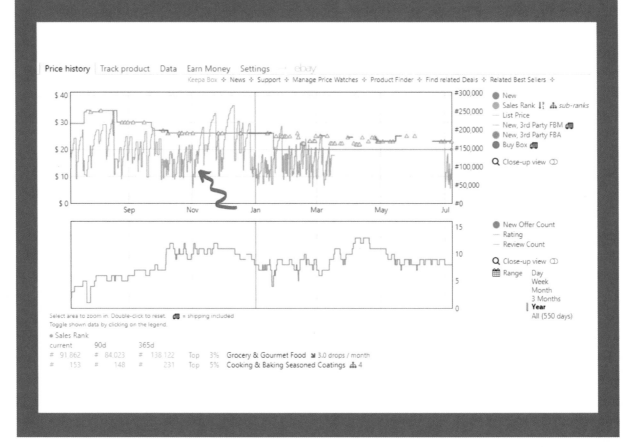

*S*ALES RANK* - Sharp drops of the green line are an indication of sales rank changes on Amazon. It may be one sale, it may be dozens; it simply indicates that sales have occurred in that time frame. A steady moving green line can be a good selling product and one to consider as a reseller.*

One possible exception to this would be if the item is a variation, so be sure to dig a bit deeper before jumping on a listing too soon from simply checking the sales rank.

Occasionally, the Sales Rank line may disappear on a Keepa graph. If it does this, you can extend the graph back further to look at the sales history or reference the Seller Count line in the bottom graph which we will explain in more detail later.

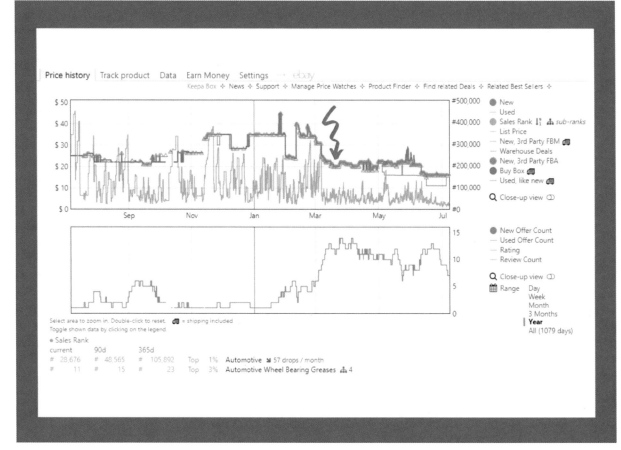

BUY BOX - *In the past, Keepa has displayed the Buy Box as pink diamonds, but it now is displayed by a pink line so pink is what you're going to be looking for here either way. Some graphs may not have this, in which case you will want to refer to the "New, 3rd party FBA" orange triangle or the "New" blue line in the top graph would be what you would be referencing.*

Keep in mind that the FBA pricing of the orange triangle is simply what the item has been listed at. It may or may not have sold at that price, so you will also need to refer to the Sales Rank green line and the Seller Count line which we'll discuss next. Also to be noted is that the New blue pricing line could be a Merchant Fulfilled price which won't necessarily include shipping fees. The Buy Box can be helpful in determining not only what the history of an item's price is, but potentially how pricing has impacted sales. As such, it is a very beneficial piece when listing your product for sale on Amazon.

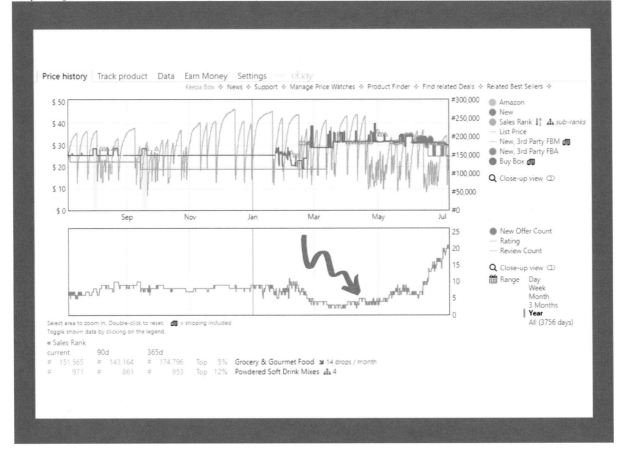

SELLER COUNT - Often referred to as the seller count, this is actually labeled as the New Offer Count on the Keepa graph. This is an important portion of the information you can gather from Keepa in a quick glance as it can quickly help you determine if the item is possibly a private label (in which case it would only have one or two sellers for an extended period of time) or if the item is actually selling. It can also be a key in deciphering if the ASIN is possibly a part of a variation listing, which you can see if the sales rank is moving quickly, but there is little to no movement of the seller count. A lot of up and down movement of the seller count can indicate sellers coming on to the listing and selling out of their stock, so without other tools it can be a useful quick resource for determining variations or sales on listings that may not have a Sales Rank line visible.

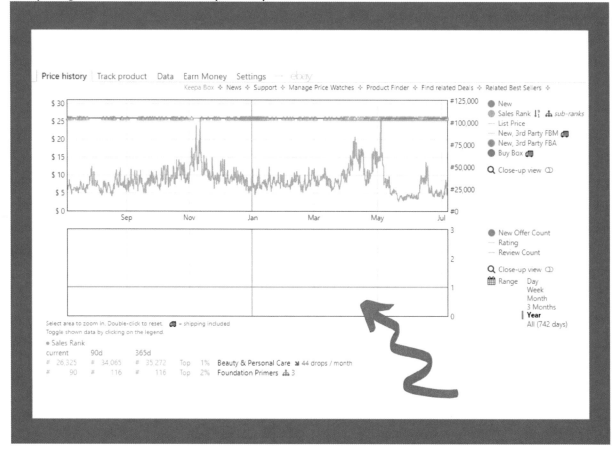

Price history | Track product | Data | Earn Money | Settings | ebay

Keepa Box ✧ News ✧ Support ✧ Manage Price Watches ✧ Product Finder ✧ Find related Deals ✧ Related Best Sellers ✧

● New
● Sales Rank ↕ ♣ sub-ranks
— List Price
— New, 3rd Party FBM 🚚
● New, 3rd Party FBA
● Buy Box 🚚
🔍 Close-up view ⬭

● New Offer Count
— Rating
— Review Count

🔍 Close-up view ⬭
📅 Range   Day
          Week
          Month
          3 Months
        | Year
          All (742 days)

Select area to zoom in. Double-click to reset. 🚚 = shipping included
Toggle shown data by clicking on the legend.

● Sales Rank

	current	90d	365d				
#	26,325	# 34,065	# 35,272	Top	1%	Beauty & Personal Care	↘ 44 drops / month
#	90	# 116	# 116	Top	2%	Foundation Primers	♣ 3

*W*hile the sales rank and buy box price both look great on this graph, here is an example of why the seller count line is an important piece of the puzzle when deciphering Keepa graphs. If you see only one seller for an extended period of time, it is a good indication of a private label or exclusive brand in which you would not be able to sell on or which could possibly trigger an intellectual property (IP) claim.

Some also choose to avoid listings that only have two sellers over an extended time as well, as there could be both an FBA listing and a MF listing. Looking at the actual Amazon listing to see who the sellers are can also give you a better idea if that is of concern or not.

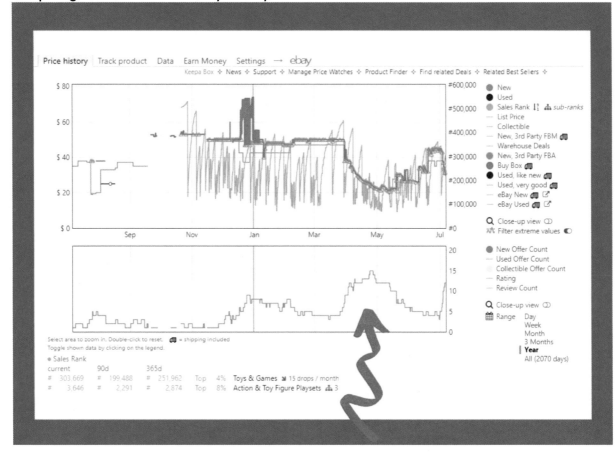

nother helpful purpose of the seller count line is to help determine potential price drops. You will notice on this particular graph that as the seller count increased, the price consequently decreased. While not always the case, this is a fairly common occurrence and something to consider if you see a drastic increase in the number of sellers on a listing. This is also a good place to point out that if you will wait for some of the sellers to sell out of their product, the price may often bounce back.

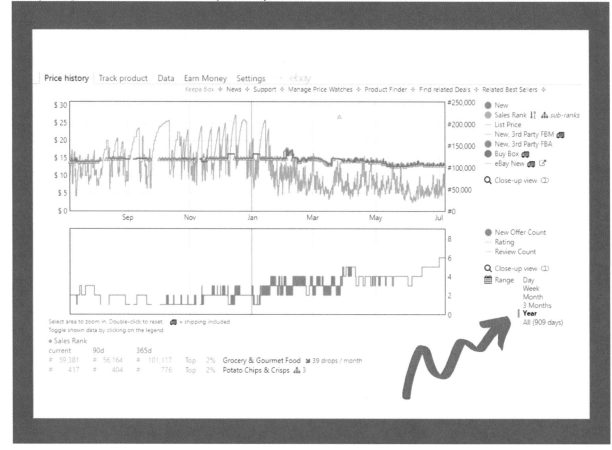

While we are pointing out the main parts of a Keepa graph, it is necessary to also point out the key to the right of the graphs. You can of course adjust your settings to fit your particular needs, but keep in mind that all of the information may not be necessary for a quick glance. If you have every feature on the graph turned on, which you can adjust by clicking next to the words, then you may risk information overload or possibly make it challenging to see the vital information you actually need to see.

Also recommended is extending the time frame of which you are looking at on the graph to at least a year, which can help determine if the item is possibly seasonal or if there have historically been other things to note.

Three quick checks on a Keepa graph

- **How often does it sell?**

- **How much is it selling for?**

- **How much competition do I have?**

ow that you have learned all of the basic parts of a Keepa graph, let's look a bit at how they help us in making better buying decisions. The answers to three simple questions can be useful in determining if an item is a wise purchase or not. For many, Keepa graphs can be overwhelming with all of the information available on them, so hopefully this will help simplify it for you.

1. *How often does it sell?*
    By watching the Sales Rank line, you can see if an item sells consistently or if it only sells seasonally or just occasionally. Depending on your business model, you can then determine if it is an item worth considering to sell.

2. *How much is it selling for?*
    While the Buy Box line only shows us what an item is listed for, not the actual sales price, it can give us a good indication if the Sales Rank is moving along with it that the item is selling for that price. Looking at the Keepa history can show us if the item has consistently sold in that price range or if it is a recent increase or decrease in the typical sales price. It can also help us to determine if the item has possibly sold at a higher velocity at a different price point. When listing and pricing your products, this can be a highly valuable bit of information.

3. *How much competition do I have?*

   This is important to know as we've already pointed out briefly. Is there only one seller consistently on the listing? Are there buyers coming on and off of the listing? Is there a sudden increase in the number of sellers? While the number of buyers alone shouldn't deter you from selling an item, you do need to be aware of how it relates to the sales velocity. If an item only historically sells once a month but has a dozen sellers on it, for example, you may want to avoid that particular item.

UNIQUE
KEEPA GRAPHS

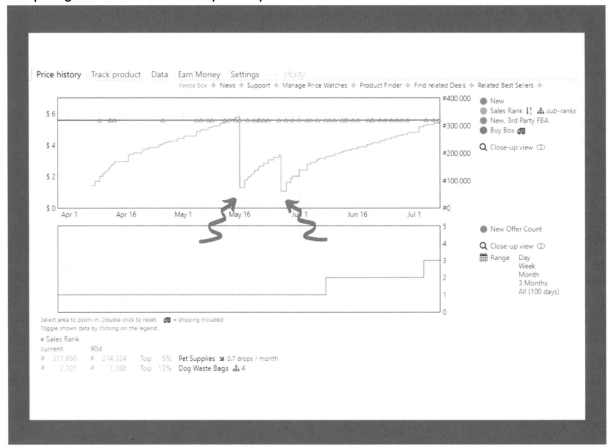

RANK ADJUSTMENTS

Keepa only provides information as it receives it from Amazon. While it is considered an excellent tool for your Amazon business, it is not without flaw. You may occasionally see graphs that look abnormal such as this one. This may look as if it has quite a few sales, but this erratic movement of the green Sales Rank line is actually not indicative of sales. These would be rank adjustments or possibly just considered a glitch. Sales Rank lines are more distinct drops, such as the two large drops on this graph, so keep this in mind when reading your graphs.

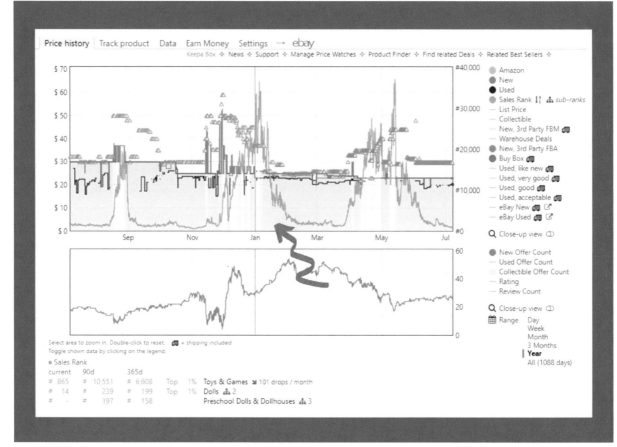

aMAZON ON THE LISTING

Oh the dreaded orange shading! Amazon is on the listing; what do you do? Most sellers avoid selling on any and all listings that Amazon is on, but you don't have to be one of them if you are able to read Keepa well. While Amazon may not share the Buy Box all of the time, there are still circumstances in which they do; and there are other things to consider when you come across a graph that looks like this.

In this particular graph, you will notice that Amazon has run out of stock quite a few times in the past year, so if you're one to take risks you may want to jump in and hope that you'll get those higher price point sales when they run out of stock next. This is a very fast moving item, so your chances are favorable for it to continue to happen.

Alternatively, you could look a bit more closely at Keepa and see if it appears that Amazon is sharing the Buy Box. One indication of that would be a lot of up and down movement of the Seller Count. This would indicate that others are coming on the listing and then running out of stock. And another way to determine this is by hovering over "Buy Box" in the key to the right and a colored line will show up at the very top of the Keepa graph, indicating colors of who was holding the Buy Box at any given time. These are just two quick, at-a-glance ways to determine if Amazon is sharing the Buy Box and may support you sending some of that product in to test.

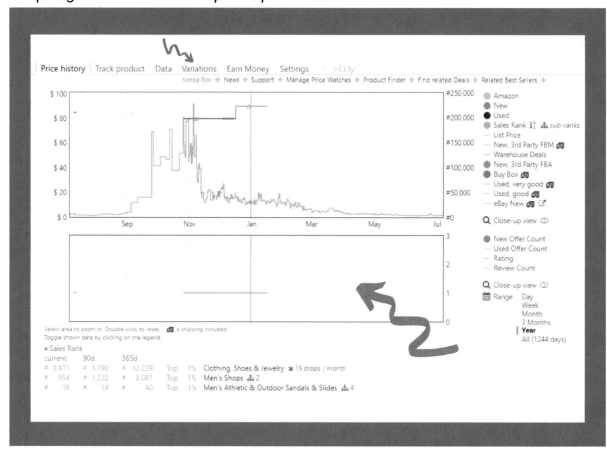

$\bigvee$*ARIATIONS*

While there may be multiple other tools that can assist in determining specifics about variations, Keepa is still a very useful tool that you can use at a quick glance to notice variations.

In this particular graph, we can see two of the three easy ways to see if an ASIN may be a part of a variation listing. One way is by observing the Variations tab at the top of the Keepa graphs. This does not appear on listings that are not variations, so that's a simple giveaway right there. Another thing we can observe in this graph is the lack of sellers in the Seller Count while the Sales Rank line is still moving quite a bit. This would indicate that another variation on this listing is receiving the sales and not this particular ASIN. A third easy way, not pictured, to recognize if an item is a variation is by small wording below the graphs by the "Sales Rank" that actually states "likely shared between all variations."

Keep in mind that simply because an item is on a variation listing does not equate to it being a poor choice when sourcing. You just need to look a bit closer at these items to determine if the ASIN you are looking at is the actual variation that is going to sell. And it doesn't hurt to test small as you're gaining confidence in your abilities to read these graphs.

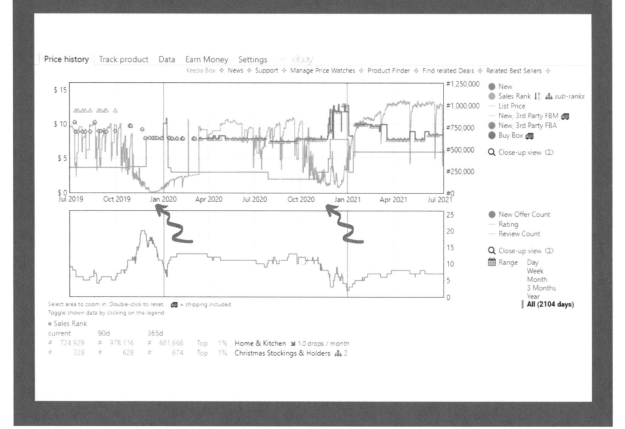

EASONAL

Earlier it was recommended to extend the range of the Keepa graph when you are evaluating an ASIN and a graph like this would be one of the reasons why. Seasonal items can often be hard to catch as good or poor sellers, depending on when you are looking at the graph. In this case of a Christmas item, you can see when the sales start to pick up and sell at a higher velocity. It may be an item you would consider sending in if you were looking in December, but if you can tell it is a seasonal item based on the Keepa history you may even consider sending it in during October if you come across it. Despite a very poor sales velocity over the summer.

Seasonal graphs can show up in a variety of seasons beyond the typical holiday season as well. Summer, Halloween, Back to School, Fall, or even meltables could be considered seasonal. If you notice a large difference in one part of a graph over another, extend it even further than a year if possible and see if it historically sells better seasonally.

KEEPA QUIZZES

Now that you've learned the basics of reading a Keepa graph, let's try out your new skills!

Would you buy this?

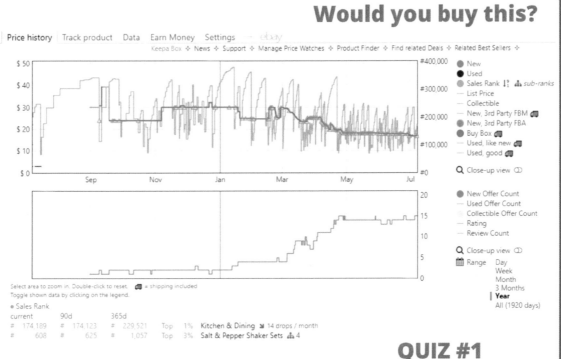

● New
● Used
● Sales Rank ↕️ 🏠 sub-ranks
— List Price
— Collectible
— New, 3rd Party FBM 🚚
● New, 3rd Party FBA 🚚
● Buy Box 🚚
— Used, like new 🚚
— Used, good 🚚

🔍 Close-up view

● New Offer Count
— Used Offer Count
   Collectible Offer Count
— Rating
— Review Count

🔍 Close-up view

📅 Range   Day
          Week
          Month
          3 Months
          Year
          All (1920 days)

Select area to zoom in. Double-click to reset.   🚚 = shipping included
Toggle shown data by clicking on the legend.

● Sales Rank
current   90d   365d
174,189   # 174,123   # 229,521   Top 1%   Kitchen & Dining ↘ 14 drops / month
608   #   625   #   1,057   Top 3%   Salt & Pepper Shaker Sets 🏠 4

QUIZ #1

QUIZ #1 RESPONSE:

While the sales rank is consistent and this looks like a great seller, this is probably an item to pass on or to at least proceed with caution regarding. The seller count looks to be growing quite a bit and pulling the sales price down at the same time. So if you have a few clearance items you want to sell quickly, then you may decide to risk sending it in. But if you're looking for a replenishable item, you may want to wait out some sellers and see if the price goes back up.

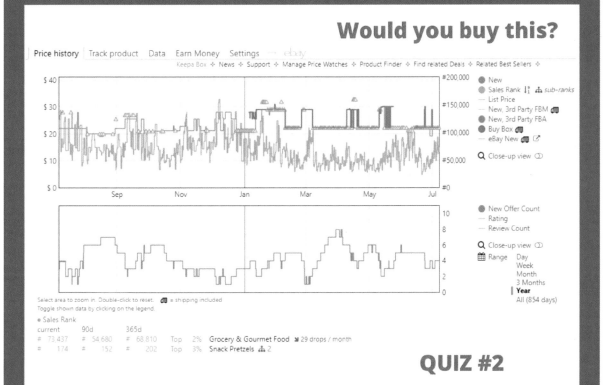

Would you buy this?

Price history | Track product | Data | Earn Money | Settings | ebay

Keepa Box ✧ News ✧ Support ✧ Manage Price Watches ✧ Product Finder ✧ Find related Deals ✧ Related Best Sellers ✧

- New
- Sales Rank ↕ ⓘ sub-ranks
- List Price
- New, 3rd Party FBM
- New, 3rd Party FBA
- Buy Box
- eBay New

Q Close-up view

- New Offer Count
- Rating
- Review Count

Q Close-up view

📅 Range   Day
Week
Month
3 Months
Year
All (854 days)

Select area to zoom in. Double-click to reset. 🚚 = shipping included
Toggle shown data by clicking on the legend.

● Sales Rank

current	90d	365d			
# 73,437	# 54,680	# 68,810	Top 2%	Grocery & Gourmet Food	↘ 29 drops / month
# 174	# 152	# 202	Top 3%	Snack Pretzels ⓘ 2	

QUIZ #2

QUIZ #2 RESPONSE:

This is a great looking Keepa graph! As long as it's profitable for you at the current price, definitely make this purchase! Consistent sales, consistent pricing, and a lot of movement of sellers would make this an ideal item to consider as a replenishable item that you can buy and sell repeatedly for your business.

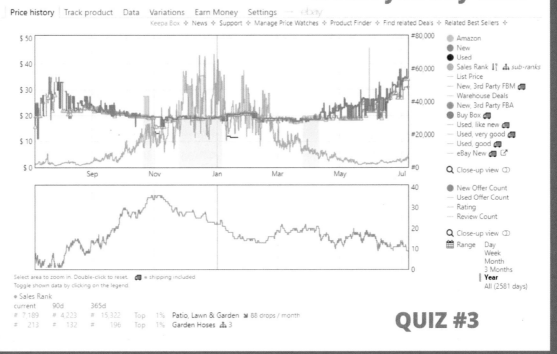

Would you buy this?

Price history | Track product | Data | Variations | Earn Money | Settings

Keepa Box ✧ News ✧ Support ✧ Manage Price Watches ✧ Product Finder ✧ Find related Deals ✧ Related Best Sellers ✧

- Amazon
- New
- Used
- Sales Rank ↓↑ ⬚ sub-ranks
- List Price
- New, 3rd Party FBM
- Warehouse Deals
- New, 3rd Party FBA
- Buy Box
- Used, like new
- Used, very good
- Used, good
- eBay New

🔍 Close-up view

- New Offer Count
- Used Offer Count
- Rating
- Review Count

🔍 Close-up view

📅 Range Day
Week
Month
3 Months
Year
All (2581 days)

Select area to zoom in. Double-click to reset. 🚚 = shipping included
Toggle shown data by clicking on the legend.

● Sales Rank

	current	90d	365d		
#	7,189	# 4,223	# 15,322	Top 1%	Patio, Lawn & Garden ⬇ 88 drops / month
#	213	# 132	# 196	Top 1%	Garden Hoses ⬚ 3

QUIZ #3

QUIZ #3 RESPONSE:

While many would avoid a listing with Amazon on the listing historically, you have learned some things in this booklet to hopefully cause you to at least consider it. In this case, Amazon is not often on the listing and the sales and pricing are fairly consistent, as is the seller count movement. If you wouldn't take a loss by selling at the Amazon pricing when they are in stock, then this would definitely be one to consider.

𝒶dditional resources for Amazon sellers and aspiring online entrepreneurs

Being an entrepreneur can often be considered a lonely path, but it doesn't need to be nor should it be. Consider joining a tight-knit community of online sellers with not only a wealth of information and resources but also an incredible list of perks for members only. Sound interesting? Here's a 30 day trial for only $1 so you can see what it's all about for yourself.
bit.ly/legends30daytrial

Often compared to a library of courses, the Proven Amazon Course is THE go-to resource for all things Amazon. Ready to expand your current Amazon knowledge exponentially? You can get started learning today for only $29.
bit.ly/PAClibrary

Just getting started in e-commerce or wanting to expand beyond your Amazon business? This is a powerful bite-sized resource that will walk you through the 3 models of online businesses and how to create multiple streams of income.
streamsofincome.com

Made in the USA
Monee, IL
28 January 2022

90158809R00026